Alexander Mellis is a barrister at No5 Chambers, specialising in personal injury work. He acts for both claimants and defendants at multi-track and fast-track level. Alexander is regularly in trial as well as undertaking the usual array of interim and case & costs management hearings, with resulting experience of the costs issues that can arise from cases that start as fixed costs cases.

A Practical Guide to Personal Injury Fixed Costs in Portal and Ex-Portal Cases

A Practical Guide to Personal Injury Fixed Costs in Portal and Ex-Portal Cases

Alexander Mellis
Barrister, MiddleTemple
LLB (Dunelm)

Law Brief Publishing

Published 2021 by Law Brief Publishing, an imprint of Law Brief Publishing Ltd
30 The Parks
Minehead
Somerset
TA24 8BT

www.lawbriefpublishing.com

Paperback: 978-1-913715-99-1

To those that convinced me to do this.

CONTENTS

INTRODUCTION

Fixed costs in personal injury are supposed to be straight forward, avoid the need for time spent on assessment and control the level of costs payable by Defendants. Whilst it usually secures those aims, there are gaps, lacunas, nuances and specific interpretations which any practitioner – be it solicitor, CILEX, paralegal, counsel or, dare I say, judge – should know.

To fully understand fixed costs, the below comments from the Court of Appeal should always be borne in mind:

> *"31. The starting point is that the plain object and intent of the fixed costs regime in relation to claims of this kind is that, from the moment of entry into the Portal pursuant to the EL/PL Protocol (and, for that matter, the RTA Protocol as well) recovery of the costs of pursuing or defending that claim at all subsequent stages is intended to be limited to the fixed rates of recoverable costs, subject only to a very small category of clearly stated exceptions. To recognise implied exceptions in relation to such claim-related activity and expenditure would be destructive of the clear purpose of the fixed costs regime, which is to pursue the elusive objective of proportionality in the conduct of the small or relatively modest types of claim to which that regime currently applies.*
>
> ...
>
> *"41. The fixed costs regime inevitably contains_swings and roundabouts, and lawyers who assist claimants by participating in it are accustomed to taking the rough with the smooth, in pursuing*

> *legal business which is profitable overall*" **Sharp v Leeds City Council**[1] per Lord Briggs (as he then was).

> "*30. The starting point is that fixed costs and assessed costs are conceptually different. Fixed costs are awarded whether or not they were incurred, and whether or not they represent reasonable or proportionate compensation for the effort actually expended. On the other hand, assessed costs reflect the work actually done. The court examines whether the costs were incurred, and then asks whether they were incurred reasonably and (on the standard basis) proportionately.*" **Broadhurst v Tan**[2] per Lord Dyson MR.

The costs are not designed to be fair in individual cases. Arguably unfair results in an individual case, against either a defendant or a claimant, are not reasons to interpret the rules differently. As such it is undoubtedly important not to miss out on recovering the costs a claimant is entitled to when they are available. Similarly, defendants will want to ensure that the aim of reducing costs payable is properly met. Understanding the 'swings and roundabouts' nature of the costs in the areas covered by this book is important to contextualise some of the judicial decisions and results of the rules, which on occasion are most certainly the 'rough' rather than the 'smooth'.

Scope

This book is aimed at everyone who deals with costs in cases which start life in the Pre-Action Protocol for Low Value Personal Injury Claims in Road Traffic Accidents ("the RTA Protocol"), the Pre-Action Protocol for Low Value Personal Injury (Employers' Liability and Public Liability) Claims ("the EL/PL Protocol") and the Pre-

[1] [2017] 4 WLR 98

[2] [2016] 1 WLR 1928

Action Protocol for Resolution of Package Travel Claims ("the Travel Sickness Protocol"). The main focus of the book is those claims that exit those Protocols, for whatever reason, together with claims under the Travel Sickness Protocol. For the RTA and EL/PL Protocols it also covers those claims where liability is admitted and that therefore stay in the Portals and either settle or go on to be determined at a Stage 3 Hearing.

A brief aside on some of the nomenclature used. The 'Portal' refers to the programme or process that the claims go through, the 'Protocol' to the rules that govern the relevant Portal.

The scope of each of these Protocols is only briefly covered. That it is included at all is primarily because it can and does sometimes arise as an issue throughout the lifetime of proceedings, even right up until the end. In that way, whilst it is generally taken as a given that the case you are dealing with falls within the fixed costs covered in this book, it would be remiss not to alert readers to the occasional issues that can arise. It is not, however, intended as a comprehensive guide to the scope of the Protocols.

The one obvious distinction that needs to be considered at the outset is that the book, or at least this first edition, does not cover the newly introduced Pre-Action Protocol for Personal Injury Claims Below the Small Claims Limit in Road Traffic Accidents ("the RTA Small Claims Protocol").

More fundamentally, for claims involving road traffic accidents after 31 May 2021 that involve personal injury damages up to £5,000 – and all whiplash injuries lasting below 2 years fall under that level due to the introduction of the Whiplash Injury Regulations 2021 – they are unlikely to fall within the scope of this book.

The RTA Small Claims Protocol is supposed to be accessible to litigants in person as well as lawyers and so it is hoped will not need to be included in a book such as this one. Time will tell if that hope proves well founded.

Some, but not all, of the rules are re-produced in full at the relevant sections of this book. Whilst familiarity with their wording and meaning is vital to accurately deploying the understanding of the rules and issues that arise from them, merely reproducing the White Book, rules or protocols would be of little benefit.

Qualified One-Way Costs Shifting ("QOWCS")

A further context that needs to be remembered throughout dealing with the issues covered by this book is Qualified One-Way Costs Shifting. It was introduced in 2013 as part of the package of reforms to control costs but maintain access to justice in personal injury claims. The rules are to be found in Part 44 rules 44.13 to 44.17. For claims not subject to a CFA before 1 April 2013, an unsuccessful claimant in a claim for personal injuries, under the Fatal Accidents Act 1976 or arising out of death or personal injury that survives for the benefit of the estate under the Law Reform (Miscellaneous Provisions) Act 1934 does not have to pay the successful defendant's costs. There are exceptions to that, most importantly if the claim is found to be fundamentally dishonest or struck out for the reasons set out at r44.15. Importantly it does not include being struck out for a failure to comply with a rule or practice direction. A further exception is where the claim is made for the financial benefit of either somebody else or includes a claim other than for personal injury, so called "mixed" claims.

A further exception is in applications for Pre-Action disclosure, per r44.13(1).

Any costs order can also be enforced where a claimant does recover damages, such as a costs award made at an interim stage or where a defendant beats their own Part 36 offer. Recoverability in those circumstances is limited to the level of damages awarded.

What is important to understand is that QOWCS does not alter the principle of what costs order should be made, only the enforceability of it.

The law described in this book was believed to be accurate on 20 July 2021.

Alexander Mellis
August 2021

PART ONE

PART 45 SECTION IIIA

CHAPTER ONE

GEOGRAPHICAL AND VAT CONSIDERATIONS

Geographical uplift

Where a party lives in an area set out in PD45 and instructs a legal representative who practices in that area, then an additional 12.5% of the costs set out in Tables 6B, 6C and 6D can be recovered per r45.29C(2) and r45.29E(2). The same is true for the fixed costs for defendant's costs per r45.29F(5) and interim hearings per r45.29H(2).

The areas may change from time to time and are specified in Practice Direction 45, but at the time of writing are as follows:

> *"the area served by the County Court hearing centres at Barnet, Brentford, Central London, Clerkenwell and Shoreditch, Edmonton, Ilford, Mayors and City of London, Romford, Wandsworth and Willesden and (outside London) the County Court hearing centres at Bromley, Croydon, Dartford, Gravesend and Uxbridge."* PD 45 para 2.6.

VAT

VAT is recoverable in addition to the figures set out in the tables, pursuant to CPR r45.29C(3) and r45.29E(3). It is also recoverable on defendant's costs per r45.29F(7) and interim costs per r45.29H(4).

CHAPTER TWO

THE FIXED AMOUNTS

This area of fixed costs is the main focus of this book. It will start with the tables that set out the costs for profit costs. The tables are deliberately reformatted, although the wording crucially remains the same, to better show the increase in costs as the case progresses through its different phases.

Save for on exception, the fixed costs set out in Section IIIA apply to all claims that started under the relevant protocols or to which the Pre-Actin Protocol for Resolution of Package Travel Claims applies, so long as they are not allocated to the multi-track {CPR 45.29B for RTA claims and r45.29D for EL/PL and Travel sickness claims}. The exception is that pursuant to r45.29A(2), the fixed costs in Section IIIA do not apply to disease claims started under the EL/PL Protocol. 'Disease claims' are as defined at paragraph 1.1 (14(b)) of the EL/PL Protocol.

In some ways the fixed costs are very simple. Costs are calculated:

- By reference to Tables 6B-6D for the costs of the claim;
- By reference to r45.29H if an interim hearing is required to take place;
- By reference to r45.29I for disbursements;
- By reference to r45.29F if the costs are for a defendant;
- By reference to r45.29G if there is a counterclaim.

The fixed costs table for RTA, EL, PL and Travel Sickness costs are found at Tables 6B, 6C and 6D respectively, with the latter table covering both PL and Travel Sickness cases.

The tables are themselves further broken down, into what we shall call sections, A-D as follows:

A. If parties reach a settlement prior to the claimant issuing proceedings under Part 7

B. If proceedings are issued under Part 7, but the case settles before trial

C. If the claim is disposed of at trial

D. Trial advocacy fees

Trial advocacy fees are the same for all types of claims, so section D for each different set of costs are found just the once after sections A-C for each type of case have been set out.

Road Traffic Accident fixed costs

These are provided for by Table 6B.

A. If parties reach a settlement prior to the claimant issuing proceedings under Part 7

Agreed damages	Fixed costs
£1,000 to £5,000	The greater of a) £550 or b) £100 + 20% of the damages
More than £5,000 to £10,000	£1,100 + 15% of damages over £5,000
More than £10,000	£1,930 + 10% of damages over £10,000

B. If proceedings are issued under Part 7, but the case settles before trial

Stage at which case is settled	Fixed costs
On or after the date of issue but prior to allocation under Part 26	£1,160 + 20% of damages
On or after the date of allocation under Part 26 but prior to the date of listing	£1,880 + 20% of damages
On or after the date of listing but prior to the date of trial	£2,655 + 20% of damages

C. If the claim is disposed of at trial

Stage	Fixed costs
If the claim is disposed of at trial	£2,655 + 20% of damages agreed or awarded + advocacy fee

<u>Employer's Liability fixed costs</u>

These are provided for by Table 6B.

A. If parties reach a settlement prior to the claimant issuing proceedings under Part 7

Agreed damages	Fixed costs
£1,000 to £5,000	£950 + 17.5% of damages
More than £5,000 to £10,000	£1,855 + £12.5% of damages over £5,000
More than £10,000	£2,500 + 10% of damages over £10,000

B. If proceedings are issued under Part 7, but the case settles before trial

Stage at which case is settled	Fixed costs
On or after the date of issue but prior to allocation under Part 26	£1,160 + 20% of damages
On or after the date of allocation under Part 26 but prior to the date of listing	£1,880 + 20% of damages
On or after the date of listing but prior to the date of trial	£2,655 + 20% of damages

C. If the claim is disposed of at trial

Stage	Fixed costs
If the claim is disposed of at trial	£4,280 + 30% of damages agreed or awarded + advocacy fee

Public Liability and Travel Sickness fixed costs

These are provided for by Table 6D.

A. If parties reach a settlement prior to the claimant issuing proceedings under Part 7

Agreed damages	Fixed costs
£1,000 to £5,000	£950 + 17.5% of damages
More than £5,000 to £10,000	£1,855 + £12.5% of damages over £5,000
More than £10,000	£2,370 + 10% of damages over £10,000

B. If proceedings are issued under Part 7, but the case settles before trial

Stage at which case is settled	Fixed costs
On or after the date of issue but prior to allocation under Part 26	£2,450 + 17.5% of damages
On or after the date of allocation under Part 26 but prior to the date of listing	£3,065 + 22.5% of damages
On or after the date of listing but prior to the date of trial	£3,790 + 27.5% of damages

C. If the claim is disposed of at trial

Stage	Fixed costs
If the claim is disposed of at trial	£3,790 + 27.5% of damages agreed or awarded + advocacy fee

The Court of Appeal explained how the sections are progressed in **Bird v Acorn Group Ltd**[3]. That case specifically dealt with how the sections are progressed in claims that are listed for disposal hearings, but the analysis applies more generally.

[3] [2017] 1 WLR 1915

The claimant, whilst at the defendant's garage to collect a new vehicle from them, had been injured when a spanner was dropped onto his hand. It was therefore a public liability claim and was started under the relevant protocol. The claim fell out of the portal when the defendant's insurers failed to respond in time. Liability was later admitted but settlement not reached and so the claim was issued. The defendant then compounded its earlier failing and also failed to respond to proceedings such that judgment in default was entered. The file was transferred to Birkenhead where it was listed for a disposal hearing. The matter settled before the hearing and proceedings compromised by way of a Tomlin Order. The costs were not agreed, the defendant asserting that only the issuing stage of section B from table 6D applied (referred to as 'column 1' within the judgment). The claimant maintained that the listing stage had been reached ('column 3' within the judgment). Briggs LJ held at [12]:

> *"In my judgment listing a case for a disposal hearing following judgment, pursuant to paragraph 12 of the Practice Direction supplementing Part 26, is listing for trial, for the purposes of triggering column 3 in Table 6D part B where a case which originated in the EL/PL Protocol settles after listing."*

In practical terms, this meant that the costs payable went up from £2,450 plus 17.5% of damages to £3,790 plus 27.5% of damages.

A further important point that flows from **Bird** is that Briggs LJ endorsed the submissions of counsel for the claimant, advanced in response to the defendant's contention that if a disposal was in fact used to set down directions there would be a need to 'backtrack' from the listing for trial:

> *"Mr Williams QC for Mr Bird had what seems to me a complete answer to it… even in a case where there was allocation to the fast track, it was common for there to be no moment in time at which column 2 applied, because rule 28.2(2)(a) provides for county court*

hearing centres to allocate to the fast track and list for trial simultaneously"[4]

Interim hearings

These are dealt with under r45.29H. Pursuant to r4529H(1) and (1A) where an order for costs is made at an interim hearing, the costs are calculated by reference to half the Type A and Type B costs in Table 6, for RTA claims, or Table 6A for, for EL/PL and Travel sickness claims. The distinction is in fact meaningless because the Type A and B costs are same in both Tables, namely £250 for each, totalling £500, and have been since their introduction. Half of £500 is of course £250. One could argue that the rule could have been expressed more simply.

Pursuant to r45.29H(3), the receiving party is also entitled to any relevant disbursements under r45.29I, most usually court fees.

The question as to what type of applications are caught by the interim hearing provisions is an important one. In **Sharp v Leeds City Council**[5] the Court of Appeal confirmed that applications for pre-action disclosure were 'interim hearings' within the scope of r45.2H. More importantly, Briggs LJ (as he then was) stated:

> *"31. The starting point is that the plain object and intent of the fixed costs regime in relation to claims of this kind is that, from the moment of entry into the Portal pursuant to the EL/PL Protocol (and, for that matter, the RTA Protocol as well) recovery of the costs of pursuing or defending that claim at all subsequent stages is intended to be limited to the fixed rates of recoverable costs, subject only to a very small category of clearly stated exceptions. To recognise*

[4]Ibid, at [21]

[5] [2017] 4 WLR 98

> *implied exceptions in relation to such claim-related activity and expenditure would be destructive of the clear purpose of the fixed costs regime, which is to pursue the elusive objective of proportionality in the conduct of the small or relatively modest types of claim to which that regime currently applies."*

Given the "*starting point*" identified by Briggs LJ, it is likely that it will be the 'end point' that most interim hearings will indeed fall within r45.29H. However, the side of the line which applications at the end of case will fall on arguably remains a little more uncertain. In **Young v AXA Insurance UK Ltd**[6] HHJ Godsmark QC determined that an application to register a judgment when a settlement under Part 36 was not paid remained an 'interim application' to which r45.29H applied.

Master Leonard in the Senior Courts Costs Office in **Nema v Kirland**[7] held at paragraph [54]:

> *"I think that Mr Waszak must be right in saying that, given that CPR 36.20 and Section IIIA of CPR 45 between them provide comprehensive, self-contained provisions for the recovery of the costs to which they apply, that* ***an application for an order under CPR 36.20(11) should be treated as an interim application under CPR 45.29H****. The application costs awarded on that basis would be modest and proportionate. I see no reason to apply the narrow interpretation of "interim application" urged on me by Mr Hogan. It seems to me that an interim application can be made at any stage before every aspect of a case is finally resolved, including on costs matters."*

---

[6] [2019] 4 WLUK 676

[7] [2019] 8 WLUK 301

By contrast, Carr J (as she then was) determined in **Parsa v DS Smith plc**[8] that an application for indemnity costs or exceptional costs under r45.29J at the end of a case was not an 'interim' application, as the word 'interim' had to mean something. As such, the defendant, who was the winning party on the application, was not restricted to costs under r45.29H.

There appears some support for the decision of Carr J in the rules themselves. CPR r45.29J(3) provides that where the court does not consider it appropriate to summarily assess or assess in detail for exceptional circumstances, it may make an order for the fixed recoverable costs of the claimant or a sum that has regard to but does not exceed the fixed costs for the defendant. Then r45.29L(1)(a) provides, insofar as is relevant, that where r45.29J(3) applies the court may:

> *"(i) decide not to award the party making the claim the costs of the costs only proceedings…; and*
>
> *(ii) make orders in relation to costs that may include an order that the party making the claim pay the costs of the party defending those proceedings or that assessment."*

It would have been simple for the rules to refer back to r45.29H if the costs ordered under the above provisions were indeed fixed by reference to that rule. Further, arguably if the risk of losing such applications came with an unknown costs exposure, save that it would almost certainly be in excess of £250 + VAT, it would be a greater incentive not to make such applications.

[8] [2019] 3 WLUK 719

Advocacy Fees

As noted, these are found in section D for all Tables 6B-6D, but as the figures are the same for each it is reproduced just once here.

D. Trial advocacy fees

Damages agreed or awarded	Advocacy fee
Not more than £3,000	£500
More than £3,000 to £10,000	£710
More than £10,000 but not more than £15,000	£1,070
More than £15,000	£1,705

There are several cases that are relevant for the determining of inter-party recovery of trial advocacy fees.

Firstly, the decision in **Bird v Acorn Group Ltd** confirms that a disposal hearing is a trial for the purposes of section D of Tables 6B-D.

Secondly, **Mendes v Hochtief (UK) Construction Ltd**[9]. On the morning of trial at court after asking for some more time from the

[9] [2016] EWHC 976 (QB)

judge to reach settlement the parties succeeded in doing exactly that. In the context of portal cases it was a sizeable settlement of £20,000 plus costs. The Recorder at first instance declined to award the trial advocacy fee on the basis that the case had settled prior to trial. Coulson J as he then was upheld the claimant's appeal, holding that the matter had not settled 'prior' to the date of trial and as such the relevant part of Table 6B that determined the costs for a claim that settled on the morning of trial was section C. Accordingly the advocacy fee was recoverable where a case settles at court on the morning trial.

What, then, about a claim that settles the day before trial? There is no binding authority on the point at the time of writing but there is Senior Courts Costs Office decision, which is likely to be highly persuasive, in **Coleman v Townsend**[10]. Master Haworth determined that where the matter had settled the day prior to the trial but counsel had undertaken a skeleton and an abated brief fee was incurred, *"the day of trial was not yet at hand"* and that accordingly the relevant section was section B. No separate fee was recoverable for counsel under Tables 6B-D. Master Haworth further held that the fee for the skeleton and the abated brief fee were not recoverable 'because of any particular feature of the dispute' under CPR r45.29(I)(2)(h). That rule is addressed more fully in the disbursement section, below.

Counterclaims

These are dealt with under r45.29G. Subparagraph (1) provides that where a defendant has a counterclaim that includes personal injury to which the RTA protocol applies, and the counterclaim succeeds, then

[10] [2020] All ER (D) 133 (Jul)

the costs of the counterclaim are the same as a claimant would ordinarily get.

The rule does not address the situation where a defendant does not put a claim into the RTA Portal themselves, but does introduce a personal injury claim when proceedings are issued. It is not for this book to suggest the answer to that situation if it were to arise. Putting aside issues of the genuineness of such a claim and the practicality of getting medical reports, it must be remembered that the original claimant's insurer would have a financial interest in the counterclaim as it would be they who would have to meet any judgment for damages and costs, even if they have no interest in the original claim themselves.

It is not unusual for insurers to take a different view of liability and wish to concede it or settle a potential claim, without prejudice to their insured's uninsured losses, such as personal injury and credit hire. The unsuccessful claimant, or their insurer, might argue that they should have at least had been given the opportunity to admit the claim within the portal and pay the counterclaim and lower costs for claims that remain within the Portal, for which see Part 2 of this book.

There is no binding authority on the status of a portal admission by an insurer if their insured then wished to bring a separate claim and it is an area of law that is outside of the scope of this book. The reader's attention is simply drawn to the County Court decision of **Chimel v Chibwana**[11] and case-law referred to therein. HHJ Simpkiss there determined that an insurer's admission in the Portal was binding on their insured but not on third parties, such as passengers of the insured.

[11] [2016] 10 WLUK 532

Where the successful counterclaim does not include personal injury, i.e. it is for insurer outlay or credit hire only, sub-paragraph 2(a) then the costs are £250 and relevant disbursements. Of note, despite having to attend a trial, the successful, non-PI counterclaimant does not recover trial advocacy fees. Presumably this is to reflect the fact that the claim would otherwise have been a small claim where such fees are also not recoverable.

Defendant costs

These are covered at CPR r45.29F. Little reference is made to this rule day-to-day because where an entirely successful defendant is subject to the QOWCS provisions, an assessment of their costs has little purpose. The more regular order is a variation on:

> *"The Claimant shall pay the Defendant's costs, not to be assessed or enforced without further order/permission of the court/leave of the court"*

An order that is silent on costs or explicitly provides 'no order for costs' is technically incorrect because, as already noted, QOWCS does not affect the *entitlement* to costs, only the *enforcement* of them.

In an odd piece of drafting, paragraph 45.29F(1) firstly sets out that that paragraphs (8) and (9) deal with where defendant's costs under Part 36 is required, then refers to paragraph (10), which applies where QOWCS exclusions apply, then jumps back to provide that paragraphs (2) to (7) otherwise apply.

Paragraph (2) provides that where a costs order in favour of a defendant is made:

> *"(a) the court will have regard to; and*
>
> *(b) the amount of costs order to be paid shall not exceed,*

> *the amount which would have been payable by the defendant if an order for costs had been made in favour of the claimant at the same stage of the proceedings."*

As such, unless the exceptions apply, the successful defendant's costs are capped by the fixed costs. They are not, however, simply entitled to the fixed costs. As to what is intended by the words "have regard to", there is at present no cases that address the issue.

Paragraph (3) addresses the fact that a wholly successful defendant will mean that the value of the claim for damages or damages will be unlikely to have been determined. As such the references in Tables 6B-D in that sense are defined as meaning 'value of the claim", which is in turn defined by paragraph (4) as:

> *(a) the amount specified in the claim form, excluding—*
>
> > *(i) any amount not in dispute;*
> >
> > *(ii) in a claim started under the RTA Protocol, any claim for vehicle related damages;*
> >
> > *(iii) interest;*
> >
> > *(iv) costs; and*
> >
> > *(v) any contributory negligence;*
>
> *(b) if no amount is specified in the claim form, the maximum amount which the claimant reasonably expected to recover according to the statement of value included in the claim form under rule 16.3; or*
>
> *(c) £25,000, if the claim form states that the claimant cannot reasonably say how much is likely to be recovered.*

It is not as clear from the wording as it could be, but it would appear that subparagraphs (4)(b) and (4)(c) remain subject to the exclusions at subparagraph (4)(a)(i) – (v), rather than total exceptions to subparagraph 4(a).

Paragraph 6 provides that a defendant is also entitled to disbursements as provided for in r45.29I, which is dealt with further below.

Paragraphs (8) and (9) provide that where a Part 36 is accepted or judgment is entered that is not more advantageous, i.e. the claimant fails to beat a defendant's offer, then the costs are dealt with at CPR r36.20 and 36.21 respectively.

Paragraph 10 provides that where the exceptions to QOWCS apply, then the defendant's costs are not assessed subject to fixed costs. This is addressed further in the Chapter 5.

CHAPTER THREE

DISBURSEMENTS

These are covered by r45.29I. It is important to note that paragraph (1) provides:

> *(1) Subject to paragraphs (2A) to (2E), the court—*
>
> > *(a) may allow a claim for a disbursement of a type mentioned in paragraphs (2) or (3); but*
> >
> > *(b) will not allow a claim for any other type of disbursement.*

British Airways v Prosser[12] confirms at [9] that CPR r44.3 that the usual tests for the assessments of costs apply to those elements of the costs that are not fixed, such as that they must be reasonably incurred, reasonable in amount and proportionate. The disbursements below should be applied with that trite point in mind.

Sub-paragraphs (2A) to (2E) deal with medical reports in whiplash claims and are dealt with further below. The disbursements allowed under paragraphs (2) and (3) are as follows:

> *(2) In a claim started under the RTA Protocol, the EL/PL Protocol or the Pre-Action Protocol for Resolution of Package Travel Claims, the disbursements referred to in paragraph (1) are*
>
> > *(a) the cost of obtaining medical records and expert medical reports as provided for in the relevant Protocol;*

[12] [2019] 1 WLR 4513

(b) the cost of any non-medical expert reports as provided for in the relevant Protocol;

(c) the cost of any advice from a specialist solicitor or counsel as provided for in the relevant Protocol;

(d) court fees;

(e) any expert's fee for attending the trial where the court has given permission for the expert to attend;

(f) expenses which a party or witness has reasonably incurred in travelling to and from a hearing or in staying away from home for the purposes of attending a hearing;

(g) a sum not exceeding the amount specified in Practice Direction 45 for any loss of earnings or loss of leave by a party or witness due to attending a hearing or to staying away from home for the purpose of attending a hearing; and

(h) any other disbursement reasonably incurred due to a particular feature of the dispute.

(3) In a claim started under the RTA Protocol only, the disbursements referred to in paragraph (1) are also the cost of—

(a) an engineer's report; and

(b) a search of the records of the—

(i) Driver Vehicle Licensing Authority; and

(ii) Motor Insurance Database.

2(a) Medical records and reports

This is largely self-explanatory, but a few comments are worthwhile. In the relevant protocols it is paragraph 7.1 – 7.8C of the RTA Protocol and paragraph 7.1 – 7.6 of the EL/PL Protocol. The Travel sickness protocol is less prescriptive compared to the others, however reference is made at paragraph 12.1 to 12.11.

The actual issue the Court of Appeal were dealing with in **British Airwars v Prosser** was whether VAT could properly be charged on the records and reports obtained by a medical reporting organisation for the solicitors and claimant. The Court confirmed that, subject to the test under CPR r44.3, they usually would be recoverable on the whole of the invoice presented by a medical reporting organisation, even where the records themselves may have come from a source that was not VAT registered.

It is an area of contention whether medical reporting organisation agency fees are always recoverable. Subparagraph (2A)(c) allows a cost of up to £30 in RTA whiplash claims for agency fees. It is not clear whether they are therefore not recoverable in EL/PL claims by virtue of the rules being silent on that issue in those sort of claims.

In **Beardmore v Lancashire County Council**[13] HHJ Wood QC allowed such agency fees in a PL claim where two invoices of £96 inclusive of VAT each were claimed, including a direct cost of £50 and £10 for each set of records and the balance being agency fees.

In **Powles v Hemmings**[14] DDJ Akers took a different view, disallowing £400 plus VAT of agency fees on an invoice for a

[13] Unreported, Liverpool County Court, 6 February 2019

[14] Unreported, St Helens County Court, 23 April 2021

psychological report, the invoice for which was £900 inclusive of VAT. The agency fees were said to be for:

> *"issuing a consent form; chasing and retrieving the completed form; issuing an instruction letter and supporting details to the expert; quality checking the medical report before sending to claimant representatives; collection and query resolution with a costs draftsman and third parties; considering claimant's expert's dates of availability and preparing correspondence to a solicitor, and so on…"*

DDJ Akers reached his decision based on the analysis in **Aldred v Cham.**[15] That case will be considered further below, but in short the Court of Appeal set out that the court should assess the nature of the work being claimed for as part of any disbursement claimed and if it arose ordinarily in a case then it would be expected to be covered by the fixed costs in Tables 6B-D and so would not be separately recoverable as a disbursement. Applying that analysis, DDJ Akers considered that the agency fee sought in **Powles** formed *"part and parcel of the fixed recoverable costs"* and were not recoverable at all.

Neither HHJ Wood QC in **Beardmore** or DDJ Akers in **Powles** appear to have had **Prosser** drawn to their attention. It was not in issue in the Court of Appeal in **Prosser** that agency fees were recoverable per se, as they would have had to have been for VAT to be charged on them at all. As it was not in issue in that case, **Prosser** is not binding on the issue of recoverability of agency fees per se, but it is likely to be highly persuasive. It is arguable that whatever the position on the recoverability of agency fees, the scale of the agency fees in **Powles**, which were more than the actual cost incurred by the psychologist for their expert report, would fall foul of being reasonable in amount, even

[15] [2020] 1 WLR 1276

if reasonably incurred *and* the ratio of **Aldred** given the types of roles that were said to be included in the agency fees.

2(b) Cost of non-medical reports

The relevant protocol references are paragraph 7.9 and 7.7 of the RTA and EL/PL Protocols respectively. It also noted at paragraph 12.3 of the Travel sickness Protocol. All 3 protocols share the wording that a report from non-medical experts will not be required in most cases but *"may be obtained where it is reasonably required to value the claim"*.

That echoes the test for the admissibility of expert evidence under Part 35 of the CPR. The case-law surrounding that is outside the scope of this work but is likely to inform the interpretation of this provision where it arises and is contentious. As the paragraphs themselves note, the occasions when such reports will be required is likely to be limited.

The wording that such reports should be obtained to *"value the claim"* gives rise to a potential issue. The protocols themselves are predicated on the assumption that liability is admitted. However, many of those cases that leave the portals do so because liability is *not* admitted. Whilst cases where non-medical expert reports are required to establish liability are also likely to be rare for cases below £25,000 in value, there is arguably a lacuna for recovering the costs of such reports. Of course, claimants will argue that they need to have an idea of the position on liability to assess the value of the claim, including any settlement value. In the absence of any authority on this point, which is likely to be rare, it will be left to judges to interpret the phrase as best they can until some form of authoritative guidance is provided in a reported case, be that at County Court level or higher.

2(c) Specialist legal advice

The relevant paragraphs are 7.10 and 7.8 of the RTA and EL/PL Protocols. There is no comparable provision in the Travel Sickness Protocol. The wording is similar in both protocols save that the reference to vehicle related damages is omitted from the EL/PL Protocol paragraph, for obvious reasons, so the extract from the RTA Protocol only is set out below,:

> *"In most cases under this Protocol, it is expected that the claimant's legal representative will be able to value the claim. In some cases with a value of more than £10,000 (excluding vehicle related damages), an additional advice from a specialist solicitor or from counsel may be justified where it is reasonably required to value the claim."*

The phrase "*vehicle related damages*" is defined at paragraph 1.1 (18) of the RTA Protocol as including pre-accident value, repair, insurance excess and hire.

In **Dover v Finsbury Food Group plc**[16] Lambert J was asked on an appeal to determine if counsel's advice awarded under (2C) was restricted to the Type C costs in Table 6 or 6A, amounting to £150. The claim had exited the EL Portal as the defendant failed to respond. Liability was later admitted and the case, originally valued at below £25,000, eventually settled for £70,000. The claimant had received advice in conference from counsel and the cost of the same, totalling £650 plus VAT, was claimed.

At first instance the defendant objected to the sum in principle and in amount. By the time the appeal reached Lambert J the argument had been refined to one that the advice was fixed at £150 by virtue of the reference to *"as provided for in the relevant protocol"* in the rule. The

[16] [2020] 1 WLR 4496

relevant EL Protocol at paragraphs 7.41 and 7.44(4) fixed the costs of such advices when the claim settled under the protocol at the £150 provided for by Table 6A Type C cost. Lambert J rejected this argument because:

> *"… paragraph 7.44 is concerned with costs recovery in a claim which has settled at Stage 2 of the Protocol, not a claim which has fallen out of the Protocol for some reason. Paragraph 7.44 falls within a section of paragraphs concerning Stage 2, including the obtaining of evidence, interim payments and submission of the Stage 2 settlement pack. The subheading of paragraph 7.44 is "settlement" obviously referring to settlement at Stage 2 and providing for the defendant paying any unpaid Stage 1 fixed costs under rule 45.18 (paragraph 7.44(2)) and the Stage 2 fixed costs under rule 45.18 (paragraph 7.44(3)). As Mr Mallalieu observed, paragraph 7.44 of the Protocol is therefore inapt when considering a claim which has fallen out of the Protocol."*

The judge also accepted that the absence of a provision fixing the cost, by contrast to the CPR r45.23B for the recoverability at Stage 3 of the cost of an advice which fixed the cost at £150, was also important. Further, the result was not absurd such as to point away from the meaning that Lambert J found arose from the wording of the rule itself.

2(d) Court fees

This is likely to be uncontroversial and follow the result of any claim or individual application. The cost of issue, hearing and issuing an application are all obvious examples. It is outside of the scope of this book to consider in any depth the arguments on whether a claimant ought to have applied for fee remission, such that the unsuccessful defendant ought not to have had to pay the relevant fee. However, it is worth noting that in the context of claims falling into Section IIIA, the issue was considered in the County Court decision of **Ivanov v Lubbe**[17]. The matter settled by way of Part 36 but the defendant argued it should not have to pay the issue fee of £455 as the unemployed claimant was likely to have been eligible for fee remission, which had not been investigated. HHJ Lethem noted at paragraphs 50 and 56:

> *"50. The core argument is whether it is reasonable to expect a Claimant to use the scheme or alternatively whether this places a burden on the taxpayer that is unreasonable. In this respect I agree with Mr. Morris that there is a loss where fee remission is utilised. The public purse is depleted by the amount that would otherwise have been paid. On this basis there is less in the public purse to devote to the justice system as a whole. Thus, any suggestion that there is not loss where fee remission is utilised is misconceived. I am satisfied that Mr. Morris is right to characterise the dispute as over who bears the loss, the public purse or the tortfeasor.*
>
> *56… it is difficult to see why a logic that applies to a Claimant who has alternative sources of funding, whether it be state (Peters), insurance (Bee v Jenson), another gratuitous source of funding (Liverpool No.2) or gratuitous support (Parry) should be different. These cases represent a formidable body of case law that allows the Claimant to legitimately elect to make their claim against the tortfeasor as opposed to relying on alternative sources of funding. Ms. Ashraf has not been able to suggest any fundamental distinction that would lead to a diametrically different decision where the loss is represented by a hearing fee as opposed to a head of damage."*

Applying that analysis, HHJ Lethem allowed the issue fee to be recovered from the defendant.

---

[17] Unreported, Central London County Court, 17 January 2020

2(e) Attendance of expert of trial

The controversial element that is likely to arise in relation to these fees are likely to be the gateway of the court having "*given permission for the expert to attend*" in a fast-track trial worth less than £25,000. The test for that gateway is set out at CPR r35.5(2), which provides:

> *2) If a claim is on the small claims track or the fast track, the court will not direct an expert to attend a hearing unless it is necessary to do so in the interests of justice.*

Where permission has been granted, the amount will be subject to the test under r44.3 that the amount is reasonable.

2(f) & (g) Witness expenses

These are dealt with together, relating as they do to what are often referred to at trial together as witness expenses. Subparagraph (f) obviously relates to those reasonable costs of travel or costs from staying away from home, such as accommodation.

Subparagraph (g) relates to loss of earnings, as specified in Practice Direction 45. The relevant cap is at paragraph 2A.1 and at the time of writing provides a cap of £95 where the value of the claim is not more than £10,000 or £135 if the value is more than £10,000.

2(h) incurred due to a particular feature of the dispute

The Court of Appeal provided the definitive interpretation of this provision in **Aldred v Cham**[18]. In that case the claimant was a child. The case fell out of the RTA Protocol due to a liability dispute, but

[18] [2020] 1 WLR 1276

the defendant eventually admitted the same and offered to settle the claim for £2,000. As the claimant was a minor the settlement required approval by the court pursuant to CPR Part 21. Approval proceedings require in most cases an advice from counsel or a solicitor supporting the settlement. This is covered by the Stage 3 Type C cost in cases which remain within the portals. However, no such provision exists in relation to claims that fall within Section IIIA.

Coulson LJ held that at [35]"

> *"Age, linguistic ability and mental wellbeing are all characteristics of the claimant regardless of the dispute. They are not generated by or linked in any way to the dispute itself and cannot therefore be said to be a particular feature of that dispute."*

Accordingly, the fact that the claimant was a child and required an approval hearing and advice as part of that was not due to the nature of the dispute and so was not recoverable. The Court of Appeal expressly apply that analysis to situations where the claimant requires a translator, such that the cost of the same, which will mean for the whole case and not just at trial, are not recoverable from the other side. It remains to be seen if a claimant will take the specific issue of the costs of translators to the Supreme Court as some form of indirect discrimination.

The Court of Appeal also went further in explaining the limits of 45.29I(2)(h) even where a disbursement arises due to a particular feature of the dispute. At [49-51] Coulson LJ analysed the matter thus:

> *"49 The scope for argument about overlap between what is recoverable under the umbrella of fixed costs, on the one hand, and what might be recoverable as a disbursement on the other, arises out of the fact that the fixed recoverable costs regime in rule 45.29C and Table 6B is based, in the main, on temporal considerations: the amount recoverable is dictated by when the case settles or is otherwise*

resolved. In order to make it workable, Table 6B cannot set out in grinding detail each and every one of the work items deemed to be included within the fixed recoverable cost at each stage: if it did, it would run to scores of pages and the disputes about any items that may have been inadvertently forgotten would be numerous. Instead it operates on the premise that all the costs which might ordinarily be expected to be incurred up to a particular stage of the case will be deemed to be included in the amount stated by way of fixed recoverable costs.

> *50. Disbursements, on the other hand, are one-o› items which are for specific items of work. They are not easily addressed by reference to the same general considerations noted above, because the need for them will depend on the particular circumstances of the case. Accordingly, the rules simply provide that where such disbursements fall into one of the categories in rule 45.29I(2) they will be recoverable in addition to the fixed costs.*
>
> *51. Applying a modicum of common sense, it seems to me that the two different concepts have been melded together in a robust and workable fashion in Section IIIA of Part 45. If an item of work is deemed (or can be said implicitly) to be within the fixed recoverable costs in Table 6B, then it will not be separately recoverable as a disbursement. The brief fee is the most obvious example of that analysis."*

Where a disbursement is claimed under 45.29I(h) it is therefore necessary to ask, firstly, what about the dispute means that it is reasonable to incur it? Secondly, does that work nonetheless fall within the fixed costs that are covered by Tables 6B-D? Accordingly, the claims for agents' fees for taking witness statements are not recoverable as the taking of statements is inherently part of the role of a solicitor and would be deemed covered by the tables.

3(a) & (b) Engineer report, DVLA and MID searches

These are largely self-explanatory. The DVLA search is likely to be useful to identify the driver and the Motor Insurance Database to identify the correct insurer to send the CNF to.

Disbursements in whiplash claims

For claims started under the RTA Protocol and involving whiplash injuries, the use and cost of medical evidence is fixed. The relevant provisions in r45.29I are set out below:

> *(2A) In a soft tissue injury claim, or a claim which consists of, or includes, a claim for a whiplash injury, started under the RTA Protocol, the only sums (exclusive of VAT) that are recoverable in respect of the cost of obtaining a fixed cost medical report or medical records are as follows—*
>
> > *(a) obtaining the first report from an accredited medical expert selected via the MedCo Portal: £180;*
> >
> > *(b) obtaining a further report where justified from an expert from one of the following disciplines—*
> >
> > > *(i) Consultant Orthopaedic Surgeon (inclusive of a review of medical records where applicable): £420;*
> > >
> > > *(ii) Consultant in Accident and Emergency Medicine: £360;*
> > >
> > > *(iii) General Practitioner registered with the General Medical Council: £180; or*
> > >
> > > *(iv) Physiotherapist registered with the Health and Care Professions Council: £180;*

(c) obtaining medical records: no more than £30 plus the direct cost from the holder of the records, and limited to £80 in total for each set of records required. Where relevant records are required from more than one holder of records, the fixed fee applies to each set of records required;

(d) addendum report on medical records (except by Consultant Orthopaedic Surgeon): £50; and

(e) answer to questions under Part 35: £80.

(2B) Save in exceptional circumstances, no fee may be allowed for the cost of obtaining a report to which paragraph (2A) applies where the medical expert—

(a) has provided treatment to the claimant;

(b) is associated with any person who has provided treatment; or

(c) proposes or recommends treatment that they or an associate then provide.

(2C) The cost of obtaining a further report from an expert not listed in paragraph (2A)(b) is not fixed, but the use of that expert and the cost must be justified.

(2D) Where appropriate, VAT may be recovered in addition to the cost of obtaining a fixed cost medical report or medical records.

(2E) In this rule, 'accredited medical expert', 'associate', 'associated with', 'fixed cost medical report' 'MedCo', 'soft tissue injury claim' and 'whiplash injury have the same meaning as in paragraph 1.1(A1), (1A), (10A), (12A), and (16A) and (20), respectively, of the RTA Protocol.

The definitions of soft tissue injury and whiplash injury are in fact mutually exclusive. Soft tissue injuries are defined the RTA Protocol at paragraph 1.1(16A) and exclude those claims which are whiplash injuries, as defined at paragraph 1.1.(20). This distinction applies to claims that arise after 31 May 2021. As noted in the introduction, for accidents after that date, the introduction of the tariff system for assessing compensation for whiplash injuries, combined with the increase in the small claims limit to £5,000 for claims after that date and the RTA Small Claims Protocol means most RTA claims that fell within the scope of Section IIIA will no longer do so.

Of particular importance for claimant solicitors is in relation to paragraph (2A), which is extracted below:

> *... the only sums (exclusive of VAT) that are recoverable in respect of the cost of obtaining a fixed cost medical report or medical records are as follows—*
>
> > *(a) obtaining the first report from an accredited medical expert selected via the MedCo Portal: £180;*
> >
> > *(b) obtaining a further report* ***where justified*** *from an expert from one of the following disciplines—*

In portal claims the words in bold have caused some controversy. In <u>**Mason v Laing**</u> HHJ Gosnell held that such reports were only justified where they fulfilled paragraph 7.8B of the RTA Protocol, which provide:

> *a further medical report, whether from the first expert instructed or from an expert in another discipline, will only be justified where—*
>
> > *(a) it is recommended in the first expert's report; and*
> >
> > *(b) that report has first been disclosed to the defendant; and*

However, HHJ Gosnell noted that:

> *"either the claimant has complied with the protocol or he has not. If he has not complied then* ***there is no provision in the protocol, so far as I am aware, where a party can seek relief from sanctions*** *and ask the court to exercise the type of discretion as is utilised under the Civil Procedure Rule 3.9 pursuant to the judgment of the Court of Appeal in Denton v White.* ***There does not seem to be a comparable situation in the protocol.***"

The *ratio* of the decision, insofar as a County Court level decision can be persuasive only, is that it is a question of compliance or not and there is no power for the court to correct or waive the error. Whilst there may not be a comparable power specified in the RTA Protocol, arguably the power is contained elsewhere.

The Practice Direction – Pre-Action Conduct and Protocols at states:

> *". Pre-action protocols explain the conduct and set out the steps the court would normally expect parties to take before commencing proceedings for particular types of civil claims"*

> *"2. A pre-action protocol or this Practice Direction must not be used by a party as a tactical device to secure an unfair advantage over another party."*

> *"13. If a dispute proceeds to litigation, the court will expect the parties to have complied with a relevant pre-action protocol or this Practice Direction. The court will take into account non-compliance when giving directions for the management of proceedings (see CPR 3.1(4) to (6)) and when making orders for costs (see CPR 44.3(5)(a)). The court will consider whether all parties have complied in substance with the terms of the relevant pre-action protocol or this Practice Direction and is not likely to be concerned with minor or technical infringements..."*

"15. Where there has been non-compliance with a pre-action protocol or this Practice Direction, the court may order that

> *(a) the parties are relieved of the obligation to comply or further comply with the pre-action protocol or this Practice Direction;*
>
> *(b) the proceedings are stayed while particular steps are taken to comply with the pre-action protocol or this Practice Direction;*
>
> *(c) sanctions are to be applied.*

16. The court will consider the effect of any non-compliance when deciding whether to impose any sanctions which may include—

> *(a) an order that the party at fault pays the costs of the proceedings, or part of the costs of the other party or parties;*
>
> *(b) an order that the party at fault pay those costs on an indemnity basis;*
>
> *(c) if the party at fault is a claimant who has been awarded a sum of money, an order depriving that party of interest on that sum for a specified period, and/or awarding interest at a lower rate than would otherwise have been awarded;*
>
> *(d) if the party at fault is a defendant, and the claimant has been awarded a sum of money, an order awarding interest on that sum for a specified period at a higher rate, (not exceeding 10% above base rate), than the rate which would otherwise have been awarded.*

Paragraph 18 then sets out the protocols currently in force, which includes the RTA Protocol without any distinction between it and any of the other protocols. There is nothing to say that the substance of paragraphs 15 and 16 do not apply to cases under the RTA protocol.

If the power exists it is arguable that the decision of **Morgan v Laing** is based on an incorrect premise.

CHAPTER FOUR

MISCELLANEOUS ISSUES

<u>Accepting Part 36 offers</u>

The Court of Appeal confirmed in **<u>Hislop v Perde</u>**[19] that where an offer is accepted out of fixed costs remain applicable. Coulson LJ stated that:

> *43. Whilst the general rule dealing with costs consequences following judgment (rule 36.17) is expressly preserved by the particular rule relating to the fixed costs regime (rule 36.21), that is not the position in relation to the rules relating to the costs consequences of accepting Part 36 offers before trial. For that situation, the general rule (rule 36.13, old rule 36.10) is not preserved by the rule applicable to fixed costs cases (rule 36.20 , old rule 36.10A). Instead, rule 36.20 makes plain that it is the only rule which applies to the costs consequences of acceptance of a Part 36offer in fixed costs cases. It preserves no part of the general rule set out in rule 36.13.*
>
> *44.... rule 36.13 itself says that it is "subject to" rule 36.20 which, because that rule applies to fixed costs cases and rule 36.13 does not, also leads to the conclusion that rule 36.13 does not apply to fixed costs cases...*
>
> *45.... the signpost in brackets after rule 36.13(1) , which makes it clear that it is rule 36.20 which "makes provision for" the relevant rules in fixed costs cases, and rule 36.13(3) , which qualifies the*

[19] [2019] 1 WLR 201

> *reference to standard costs with the words "except where the recoverable costs are fixed by these Rules".*

It is clear from the judgment that this was not really even a case of interpreting the rules and clarifying their meaning with a judicial gloss. Rather the rules themselves, as Coulson LJ set out, lead to that clear result.

In relation to defendant costs where a claimant accepts an offer out of time, CPR r36.20(12) contains the now familiar formulation that:

> *Where the court makes an order for costs in favour of the defendant—*
>
> *(a) the court must have regard to; and*
>
> *(b) the amount of costs ordered must not exceed,*
>
> *the fixed costs in Table 6B, Table 6C or Table 6D in Section IIIA of Part 45 applicable at the date of acceptance, less the fixed costs to which the claimant is entitled under paragraph (4) or (5).*

<u>Multiple claimants: all personal injury</u>

The rules do not explicitly deal with the situation where there are multiple claimants within a case. The practice seems settled that each claimant is entitled to the fixed costs in relation to their claim, although how to approach the advocacy fee in Section D of Tables 6B-D (although the issue primarily arises in relation to RTA claims and Table 6B) remains more variable.

In **Neary & Neary v Bedspace Resource Ltd**[20] HHJ Pearce determined that each claimant was entitled to their own fixed costs, including advocacy fee, since:

> *"Under the protocol there is no possibility of including the claim of more than one injured person in one claim. The protocol provides for a claim notification form which can only relate to a single person, and the throughout the protocol the assumption is that only a single Claimant is involved. Table 6B cannot in my judgment properly be interpreted to mean the costs of the claim in any more broad sense than that contemplated by the protocol, that is to say the cause of action of an individual."*

That case also included an example of recoverability of counsel's fees for a conference as a disbursement reasonably incurred due to a particular feature of the dispute given that *"the Defendant came close to (though did not) allege fraud"*.

In **Karnicka v Zborek**[21] HHJ Hand QC agreed that so far as profit costs were concerned, each claimant was separately entitled to fixed costs under Table 6B. However, the advocacy fees in section D of Table 6B were not separately recoverable for each claimant. In such circumstances HHJ Hand QC held that the advocacy fee was recoverable on the basis of the combined total of damages recovered. He reached his decision in part by analogy with CPR Section VI r45.40, which is a section headed 'Fast Track Trial Costs'.

Which approach is the 'correct' one will remain in need of binding authority.

---

[20] [[2015] 12 WLUK 170

[21] [2018] 2 WLUK 295

The extent to which reference to other parts of the CPR can be made remains unclear. HHJ Hand QC stated *"I am not prepared simply to shrug my shoulders and say that what happens in one context is irrelevant to another"*. In **Aldred v Cham**, the Court of Appeal was also split on the issue. Coulson LJ gave the leading judgment and stated at [59] that:

> *"59. In arriving at my interpretation of the relevant rule, it has been unnecessary for me to have regard to anything other than the applicable part of the fixed costs regime, namely Section IIIA. As I have already indicated, I am not persuaded by the utility of the "compare and contrast" exercises… In my view, the parties should focus on the rules that cover their particular dispute: it is neither practicable nor necessary to argue about the recoverability of an item of cost worth £150 by reference to lengthy Sections of the CPR which, on any view, apply at best tangentially to the dispute that has arisen."*

By contrast the other two members of the court disagreed. McCombe LJ, with whom Nicola Davies LJ agreed, stated at [72]:

> *"It seems to me that in matters affecting the proper construction and meaning of the CPR (as of any other enactment), it is impossible to approach the matter in discrete compartments. It is necessary to construe any such instrument as a whole. I do not think that comparisons between the wording of the various Sections of Part 45 of the Rules will always be avoidable. Nor do I think that such comparisons are unhelpful. It is necessary that the CPR and, even more so, particular Parts of them are approached and interpreted as a coherent whole. The fixed costs rules should not be allowed to hold within their various Sections divergent meanings for essentially similar words."*

Multiple claimants: one in portal, one not

A vehicle owner who was not in the vehicle at the time or not injured will not fall within Section IIIA. Setting aside the ability of a bailee in possession to potentially bring vehicle related damage claims, which is outside of the scope of this book, it means that there may be a personal injury claim that is within Section IIIA and an additional claim that is not.

Obviously the uninjured claimant is not entitled to fixed costs under Section IIIA. The claim may have been a small claim but for the personal injury claim of the other claimant, which arguably would bear more relationship to the situation and costs of the non-personal injury counterclaim. On the other hand, the claim was allocated to the fast-track and so that costs regime applies unless reallocated.

There is also the issue of the correct advocacy fee. Arguably their advocacy fee, if separately recoverable per **Neary**, would fall into Section VI, which provides slightly different figures for counsel's fee. If not separately recoverable, per **Karnicka**, the slightly different figures between PI and non-PI cases may make the aggregated value of damages recovered yet more controversial.

The correct approach will again be up to the individual judge in the absence of any binding authority.

Failure to recover more than the small claims limit

It is a gateway to the Portals and for the Travel Sickness Protocol that the small claims track would not be the normal track for the claim.[22] What, then, when settlement or judgment is for a sum that would mean that the small claims track would have been the correct track?

Conlon v Royal Sun Alliance Plc[23] is authority for the proposition that a court can re-allocate a claim even after judgment, if there is a good reason to do so. HHJ Pearce did that in **Kavak v FMC Chemicals Ltd**[24] after he had dismissed a claim for personal injury but allowed vehicle damages, which would have put the claim on the small claims track in terms of value allowed in the judgment. The claimant was also found not to be dishonest. The judge determined that the personal injury claim should never have been brought, as the claimant had been involved in 2 previous accidents which had caused symptomatic injuries that remained at the time of the index accident. The claimant in his evidence accepted he could not say whether the injuries were worse because of the index accident or if it was the continuing effects of the previous accidents.

That of course runs against the wording of rules r45.29B and 45.29D that provide for cases started under the protocol "*the only costs allowed*" are those under Section IIIA. Section IIIA continues to apply save for the specified exceptions unless the claim was allocated to the multi-track. As was noted in **Sharp v Leeds City Council** and reaffirmed in **Aldred v Cham**, the fixed costs are part a regime that is of a *"comprehensive nature"* with inevitable *"swings and roundabouts"*.

22 paragraph 4.1(4) of both the RTA Protocol and EL/PL Protocol and 4.1(5) of the Travel Sickness Protocol

23 [2015] 2 WLUK 810

24 [2018] 4 WLUK 413

Parties should also be aware of CPR r46.13 which provides that:

> *(2) Where –*
>
> > *(a) claim is allocated to a track; and*
> >
> > *(b) the court subsequently re-allocates that claim to a different track,*
>
> *then unless the court orders otherwise, any special rules about costs applying –*
>
> > *(i) to the first track, will apply to the claim up to the date of re-allocation; and*
> >
> > *(ii) to the second track, will apply from the date of re-allocation.*
>
> *(3) Where the court is assessing costs on the standard basis of a claim which concluded without being allocated to a track, it may restrict those costs to costs that would have been allowed on the track to which the claim would have been allocated if allocation had taken place.*

The court will therefore need to be aware the re-allocating does not itself remove the entitlement to costs in Section IIIA, rather an additional order is likely to be needed. If the power to order costs other than those in Section IIIA does exist in circumstances where a judgment figure is less than the small claims track limit, then it is likely to require a focus on the decision to value the claim at more than the small claims track limit and the reasonableness of that at the time the decision was taken.

Deceased claimant

The Court of in **West v Burton**[25] confirmed that where the claim was sent to the defendant and then exited the RTA Protocol, the injured party then died but the claim later settled having been pursued by the executor of the estate, the correct costs were those under CPR Section II, not Section III. Sir Nigel Davis, giving the lead judgment, stated at [39]:

> *"Read as a whole, the Rules and the Protocol are, in my opinion, drafted on the footing that the claimant throughout remains the person who issued the CNF… for the purposes of the Protocol, the claimant throughout is regarded as the person who was involved in the road traffic accident.*

Appeal

In **Blair v Wickes Building Supplies Ltd (No2)**, after an unsuccessful second appeal in a portal case, i.e. costs falling under Section III rather than IIIA, the claimant contended that the costs remained fixed. The Court of Appeal held at [24]:

> *"…the fixed costs regime applicable to proceedings at first instance under the Protocol does not apply to the costs of an appeal. Instead, the appellate court has a discretion in such cases to limit the costs recoverable."*

Appellate courts do have a power to limit costs under CPR r52.19(1) where at first instance costs were limited or excluded. A party will therefore need to apply for such a power to be exercised if it wishes costs to be restricted.

[25] [2021] EWCA Civ 1005

It is likely a similar analysis applies to Section IIIA cases.

Applications to determine costs

In **Ho v Adelekun** Newey J stated:

> *"CPR Pt 45 does not itself explain how the amount recoverable in respect of disbursements under r.45.29I is to be determined, but it was common ground between counsel that the provisions relating to detailed assessment found in CPR Pt 47 would apply. Mr Roy illustrated the point by reference to Aldred v Cham. That case involved an issue as to whether a fee in respect of advice from counsel was within the fixed costs regime in Section IIIA of Pt 45. As can be seen from [8] and [9] of the judgment of Coulson LJ, the matter was the subject of first a provisional assessment and then an oral assessment, in accordance with CPR r.47.15."*

That was the result of agreement between counsel, rather than determined by the Court of Appeal after argument.

By contrast, the Senior Courts Costs Office in **Mughal v Higgs & EUI Ltd**[26] and **Nema v Kirkland**[27] together with HHJ Lethem in **Ivonov v Lubbe**[28] all accepted that the receiving party should make an application under Part 23 for an order under CPR r36.20(11). That rule states *"Where the parties do not agree the liability for costs, the court must make an order as to costs."* Those judges all accepted that there was no deemed costs order from a settlement in the fixed costs regime sufficient to give rise to a right to detailed assessment.

[26] Unreported, 6 October 2017, Master Haworth

[27] [2019] 8 WLUK 301, Master Leonard

[28] Unreported, Central London County Court, 17 January 2020

Which is the correct approach remains subject to a decision after reasoned argument on the issue, potentially up to Court of Appeal level.

Payment of Stage 1 and 2 costs

An often-overlooked rule is CPR r45.28. that provides that where a claim leaves the relevant protocol that a court, when making any costs order, *"take into account the Stage 1 and Stage 2 fixed costs that have been paid by the defendant."* The rule specifically provides that it applies with costs orders under Section II or Section IIIA.

Set-off

The Court of Appeal in **Howe v Motor Insurers' Bureau (Costs)**[29] and again in **Ho v Adelekun (Costs)**[30], confirms that there is a power to order set-off a defendant's costs against a claimant's costs under r44.12. Those cases specifically addressed the set off of appeal costs in the defendant's favour against the substantive costs awards in the substantive litigation in the claimant's favour. This is because set-off is not a form of enforcement which is what QOWCS prevents. Whilst the principle is wider of application, the Court of Appeal urged the Rules Committee to consider the matter further.

[29] [2020] Costs LR 297

[30] [2020] Costs LR 317

CHAPTER FIVE

EXCEPTIONS AND ESCAPES FROM FIXED COSTS

The only way to escape the fixed costs regime which would otherwise apply are:

- Allocation to the multi-track
- Arguing the claimant's costs should be restricted under r45.24.
- By beating a Part 36 at trial;
- Contracting out of fixed costs when settling the claim;
- Arguing 'exceptional circumstances' under r45.29J;
- The exceptions provided for defendants under r45.29F(10);

Multi-track allocation

CPR r45.29B and r45.29D now expressly provide that when allocated to the multi-track fixed costs in Section IIIA cease to apply. The Court of Appeal had to correct the initial omission of this escape from the fixed costs regime in **Qader v Esure Services Ltd**[31]

[31] [2017] 1 WLR 1924

Restriction to Portal costs r45.24

CPR r45.29A(3) provides that Section IIIA is subject to CPR r45.24, which gives the court a power to restrict a claimant's costs where the claimant did not comply with the relevant Protocol or elects not to continue with it and starts proceedings under Part 7 {(r45.24(1).

The court may, and so has a discretion, restrict a claimant to costs under r44.18 and r44.19 where:

> The defendant did not proceed with the protocol process due to insufficient information in the CNF: per r45.24(2)(a)
>
> The claimant unreasonably: r45.24(2)(b)
>
> i. Discontinued the process under the relevant protocol
>
> ii. Valued the claim at more than £25,000 and did not comply with the protocol
>
> iii. In any other way caused the protocol process to be discontinued
>
> The claimant did not comply with the protocol at all despite falling within it: r45.24(2)(c).

The court may also not order the defendant to pay the claimant's costs and disbursements save in exceptional circumstances where the claimant did not include the unique reference number provided from a search of the askCUEPI website on the CNF, per r45.29(2A).

Portal costs where the matter settles

The power under r45.24 is, however, only applicable after a judgment has been provided, per the wording of 45.24(2) that starts *"where a judgment is given in favour of the claimant..."* (emphasis added). That the rule cannot be re-written was confirmed in **Williams v Secretary of State for Business, Energy & Industrial Strategy**[32]. There the CoA upheld the decision of HHJ Godsmark QC that where a matter had settled that had incorrectly not commenced in the EL Portal, the costs judge to hold the claimant was restricted to Portal costs simply because of r45.24. That required the re-writing of r45.24. The Court of Appeal went further. The warnings within the EL Protocol on failing to comply combined with the r44.4 'Factors to be taken into account in deciding the amount of costs' and r44.11 'Court's powers in relation to misconduct' meant that a defendant should argue the costs should nonetheless be assessed by reference to the portal costs only.

Beating a Part 36 offer

The outcome in this situation can be relatively shortly stated but the analysis is a little more complex, not least because the numbering of Part 36 has changed since the leading case was decided.

Where a Claimant beats their Part 36, i.e. *"judgment against the defendant is at least as advantageous to the claimant as the proposals contained in a claimant's Part 36 offer"*,[33] then they are entitled to the staged costs in Tables 6B-D up until the point that the offer expired and then indemnity costs thereafter, i.e. without reference to the fixed costs.

[32] [2018] 4 WLR 147

[33] CPR r36.17(1)(b)

This is the result of the decision in **Broadhurst v Tan**[34] where the Court of Appeal held that the then predecessor of what is now r36.17(4)(b) took precedence over r45.29B for RTA claims (and by the same analysis r45.29D for EL/PL and Travel Sickness claims). Lord Dyson MR held at [25], with the rules now in force inserted into the quote:

> *"The effect of rules* [36.17] *and* [36.21] *when read together is that, where a claimant makes a successful Part 36 o›er, he is entitled to costs assessed on the indemnity basis. Thus, rule* [36.17] *is modified only to the extent stated by* [36.21]. *Since rule* [36.17(4)] *has not been modified by rule* [36.21], *it continues to have full force and effect. The tension between rule 45.29B and rule* [36.14A] *must, therefore, be resolved in favour of rule* [36.21]*."*

Lord Dyson went on to note at [26], with the similar amendments to the original judgment:

> *"Rule* [36.21(10)] *provides further support for my conclusion. This provision states that in a Section IIIA case the parties (i.e. claimant as well as defendant) are entitled to disbursements allowed in accordance with rule 45.29I in any period for which costs are payable to them. This reflects rule 45.29B(b). If, as Mr Laughland contends, rule 45.29B prevailed over rule* [36.21] *in any event, this provision would have been unnecessary. It is significant that rule* [36.21] *does not contain a provision which reflects rule 45.29B(a) and 45.29C. In my view, the fact that rule* [36.21] *contains provision for payment of disbursements in accordance with rule 45.29B(b), but not for payment of fixed costs in accordance with rule 45.29B(a) confirms that the interpretation that I have adopted above is correct."*

[34] [2016] 1 WLR 1928

Defendant beats own Part 36 offer

Broadhurst v Tan does not apply to defendant offers. Rather the rules themselves deal with the issue at r36.21(2(a), which provides:

> *... where an order for costs is made pursuant to rule 36.17(3)—*
>
> *(a) the claimant will be entitled to the fixed costs in Table 6B, 6C or 6D in Section IIIA of Part 45 for the stage applicable at the date on which the relevant period expired; and*
>
> *(b) the claimant will be liable for the defendant's costs from the date on which the relevant period expired to the date of judgment.*

In relation to those costs provided in subparagraph (b), r36.21(9) provides:

> *Where the court makes an order for costs in favour of the defendant—*
>
> *(a) the court must have regard to; and*
>
> *(b) the amount of costs ordered shall not exceed,*
>
> *the fixed costs in Table 6B, 6C or 6D in Section IIIA of Part 45 applicable at the date of judgment, less the fixed costs to which the claimant is entitled under paragraph (2) or (3).*

Reference must also be made back to r36.17(3) that where a claimant fails to obtain a judgment more advantageous than a defendant's Part 36 offer

> *the court must, unless it considers it unjust to do so, order that the defendant is entitled to—*

(a) costs (including any recoverable pre-action costs) from the date on which the relevant period expired; and

(b) interest on those costs.

That rule is to be contrasted with r36.17(4)(b), which provides a claimant is entitled to *indemnity* costs from the date of expiry. Accordingly, the assessment of a defendant's costs are not on the indemnity basis.

It is worth drawing attention to an oddity in the drafting of Part 36 in relation to soft tissue injury claims. The relevant rules are as follows:

36.17(8) Paragraph [36.17]*(3) does not apply to a soft tissue injury claim to which rule 36.21 applies.*

36.21(2) Subject to paragraphs (3), (4) and (5), where an order for costs is made pursuant to rule 36.17(3)—

(a) the claimant will be entitled to the fixed costs in Table 6B, 6C or 6D in Section IIIA of Part 45 for the stage applicable at the date on which the relevant period expired; and

(b) the claimant will be liable for the defendant's costs from the date on which the relevant period expired to the date of judgment.

36.21(4) In a soft tissue injury claim, if the defendant makes a Part 36 offer or Protocol offer before the defendant receives a fixed cost medical report, paragraphs (2) and (3) will only have effect in respect of costs incurred by either party more than 21 days after the defendant received the report.

Putting them together, the rule (36.17(3)) providing for a defendant's costs where a defendant Part 36 is not beaten is said not to apply to soft tissue injury claims (36.17(8)), but then in r36.21(4) for soft tissue injury claims it is said that am order under 36.17(3) is calculated by reference to 36.21(2) with the amendment of such an order only applying to either party's costs 21 days after a fixed costs medical report is received. It would appear that the wording of r36.17(8) is incorrect insofar as it seeks to disapply 36.17(3) entirely, rather it is supposed to make r36.17(3) and r36.21(2) subject to r36.21(4). This is of course entirely subject to confirmation or disagreement in any judicial decision.

Offer made less than 21 days before trial

It occasionally arises that Part 36 offers are made less than 21 days before trial and then beaten. Parties should be aware of r36.17(7)(c) which provides that the automatic costs consequences of beating a Part 36 do not apply unless the court abridges time.

Exceptional circumstances: CPR r45.29J

This is a concept easier stated than applied. It will likely be easy to spot an 'exceptional' case when it arises than to try and define what makes a case exceptional.

The Court of Appeal briefly discussed 'exceptional circumstances' in **Hislop v Perde** at [53-57]. Whilst accepting that "*it remains the position that, in an exceptional case of delay, it may be possible for the claimant to escape the fixed costs regime*"[35], Coulson LJ went on to state that:

> "*55. First, I do not consider that a defendant s late acceptance of a claimant s Part 36 o›er can always be regarded as an exceptional*

[35] Per Coulson LJ at [53]

> *circumstance. On the contrary, I take the view that my reasoning in* Fitzpatrick's case [2010] 2 Costs LR 115 *as to why there can be no <u>presumption</u> in favour of indemnity costs in these circumstances (see para 37 above) is also applicable, at least in general terms, to the suggestion that there is a <u>presumption</u> that a late acceptance of a Part 36 offer is an exceptional circumstance for the purposes of rule 45.29J…*
>
> *57. … It goes without saying that a test requiring exceptional circumstances is already a high one…"*

However, Coulson LJ stated at [54] that he was "*anxious not to express detailed conclusions about the scope and extent of rule 45.29J because, other than acknowledging that it provides a potential escape route in an appropriate case, I do not consider that its general ambit is directly relevant to this appeal.*"

The main case, therefore, that grapples with the concept of 'exceptional circumstances' is **<u>Ferri v Gill</u>**.[36] The claimant was injured riding his bike. The claim was initially intimated on the RTA Portal but the claimant later changed solicitors, who told the defendant that they did not consider it a "fast track portal claim" and they would run the matter accordingly. The claim eventually settled for £42,000 prior to the issue of proceedings. The Master at first instance applied a 'low bar' test of exceptionality against the 'basket of cases' that would be in the portals and accordingly found exceptional circumstances.

Applying the dicta of **<u>Hislop</u>**, quote above, Stewart J noted that the 'low bar' test was incorrect. The judge accepted that the Master had meant the basket included cases both in the portals *and* those that had exited it. However, the correct comparison was only with those cases that held exited the portals, for whatever reason.

---

36 [2019] Costs LR 367

There is potentially a tension between **Ferri** and **Parsa v DS Smith Plc**[37] as Carr J (as she then was) held "*the application of CPR 45.29J is always going to be a highly contextual exercise and fact-specific; there is little to be gained from comparisons with the facts of other cases*". The cases were determined at a similar time and although Stewart J was aware of Carr J's decision, no report was then available. It will have to await a further decision to see if there is a tension and whether it has any practical impact upon such applications.

Master Leonard in the Senior Courts Cost Office in **Hammond v SIG Plc**[38] also declined to find exceptional circumstances in a claim that, whilst initially indicated to be in excess of the RTA Portal limit and so started by a Letter of Claim, then had a CNF sent in accordance with the protocol. The case exited and was issued but settled for £36,500 before allocation. Both the defendant's invitation to send a CNF and the settlement amount were held by the Master not to amount to exceptional circumstances.

The Master was referred to a decision of **Jackson v Barfoot Farms**[39]. There the claim settled for £350,000, shortly before **Qader** was handed down, which dispelled any ideas that Section IIIA fixed costs did not apply to claims over £25,000. Whilst the agreement on costs did not, the judge found, amount to a contractual agreement to displace fixed costs, the lack of knowledge of what **Qader** would determine together with displacement of erroneous industry practice was unusual. Finally, the eventual complications and settlement sum meant it was *"difficult to think or a more clear-cut case of exceptional circumstances"*. The reality is probably that **Jackson** merely shows some cases are indeed easy to identify but does not otherwise assist in

---

37 [2019] 3 WLUK 719

38 [2019] 6 WLUK 151

39 Unreported, Canterbury County Court, DJ Jackson 29 November 2017

understanding 'exceptional circumstances'. Certainly, Master Leonard agreed with the outcome but did not find it helpful beyond that.

Before leaving this issue, one further case can be mentioned. In **West v Olakanpo** the claimant had made a Part 36 that was accepted late. The defendant denied his vehicle was even present, but nonetheless the matter was settled. The claimant applied for exceptional costs on the basis of the defendant's dishonesty. Robin Knowles J allowed an appeal as the judge reached the decision on the defendant being dishonest in inappropriate circumstances, but noted that "*There is no difference on this appeal between Mr Edmondson, for the claimant, and Mr Roger Mallalieu QC, for the defendant, that dishonesty is capable of being an exceptional circumstance*". Whilst that was not decided by the court, being the subject of a concession, it was an obvious one to make. As the facts of **West** show, however, reaching that determination where the matter has settled rather than been determined at trial in the usual way may yet prove more difficult.

Costs of the exceptional circumstances assessment

This is dealt with under rules 45.29J to L.

Of importance, r45.29K means that if a party fails to improve upon the fixed costs by 20%, excluding VAT, then the court will either order the payment of the fixed costs, even if the assessed costs were higher, just not more than 20% higher. Further, if somehow the assessed costs come out as *less* than fixed costs, the lower assessed costs figure is the one that the paying party will be ordered to pay.

It is then provided for by r45.29L that where the original application for fixed costs is not successful or the assessed costs are less than a 20% improvement on the fixed costs, the court may disallow the costs of the party applying for the exceptional costs and order them to pay the other party's costs of the assessment.

Contracting out of fixed costs

In **Ho v Adelekun**[40] Newey LJ stated at [12] that:

> "*On the other hand, there is no bar on contracting out of the fixed costs regime. In Solomon v Cromwell Group Plc, Moore-Bick LJ spoke at [21] of parties being unable to recover more or less by way of costs than is provided for under the fixed costs regime "subject to any agreement between the parties to the contrary".*

However, he went on to state at [30] that:

> "*If, therefore, a party to a claim that no longer continues under the RTA Protocol offers to pay costs on a basis that departs from Pt 45, the offer will be incompatible with Pt 36 and cannot be an offer under that Part...*"

It is therefore apparent that it is technically possible to contract out of the fixed costs regime, although it cannot be done by way of an offer that purports to be a Part 36. However, that had not occurred in **Ho**. Although the offer letter referred to the defendant paying costs pursuant to CPR r36.13, i.e subject to assessment on the standard basis, that rule sent fixed costs cases to CPR 36.20 and the fixed costs provisions. Further, references to "detailed assessment" was itself not sufficient to displace the intention of making a compliant Part 36 offer and the effect of the wording of r36.13 itself.

---

[40] [2019] Costs LR 1963

Where the QOWCS exceptions apply: r45.29F(10)

The exceptions are set out at CPR r44.15 and r44.16 but in brief are:

Struck out, r44.15(1)

a) for disclosing no reasonable grounds for bringing the claim;

b) the proceeding are an abuse of process;

c) the conduct of the claimant or a person acting on the claimant's behalf with the claimant's knowledge of the conduct, is likely to obstruct the just disposal of the proceedings

or

a) the claim is found to be fundamentally dishonest, per 44.16(1);

b) includes a claim for the financial benefit of somebody other than the claimant or a dependant, save for gratuitous provision of care, subrogated claim for earnings or medical expenses, per r44.16(2)(a);

c) a claim is made for the benefit of the claimant other than a claim to which this QOWCS applies, per 44.16(2)(b)

Where paragraph (2)(a) applies the court may make the costs order against the person for whom the financial benefit was claimed, subject to the mechanisms required under CPR r46.2.

PD44 paragraph 12.2 provides credit hire and subrogated claims as examples which are made for the financial benefit of others. See **Select**

Care Rentals (Noth West) Ltd v Esure Services Ltd[41] for an example of the exception being applied and upheld on appeal.

For the circumstances in which the 'mixed claims' exception in paragraph 2(b) may apply, see Commissioner of Police for the Metropolis v Brown[42].

It also worth noting that PD44 paragraphs 12.4(c) & (d) provide that where a claim is discontinued the court may direct the issue of fundamental dishonesty to be determined without setting aside that discontinuance. In such circumstances the court may determine the costs attributable to the claim having been found to be fundamentally dishonest as it thinks just and reasonable.

41 [2017] 1 WLR 4426

42 [2020] 1 WLR 1257

PART TWO

PORTAL COSTS

CHAPTER SIX

PART 45 SECTION III

Portal Costs Stages 1 – 3

The Portals in outline

The costs payable in these cases can only be understood once the structure of Portals is understood. This section only applies to cases that take place under the RTA Protocol and EL/PL Protocol.

In this chapter, references in the form [RTA number] or [EL/PL number] are to paragraphs within the named protocol.

The Stages

Stage 1 – Claimant sends a Claims Notification Form ("CNF"). If Defendant admits liability, the parties proceed to Stage 2.

Stage 2 – Claimant provides a Stage 2 settlement pack with medical evidence and other supporting evidence, containing their offers for each head of loss. The Defendant counter-offers and the parties negotiate. If the parties settle, the claim ends at Stage 2. If not, both parties make their final offers and proceed to Stage 3.

Stage 3 – the Claimant issues a claim pursuant to Practice Direction 8B. The court determines the claim at a Stage 3 hearing, either on the papers alone or having heard submissions from the parties.

At Stage 3 there are 3 sets of potential costs in addition to any disbursements. These are:

Type A – legal representative's costs.

Type B – advocacy costs where the case is decided at a hearing with submissions, rather than on the papers.

Type C – advice costs where the Claimant is a child.

Where settlement is not reached at Stage 2 the Claimant creates a Court Proceedings Pack. This is made up of two sections; Part A which is a table that the judge sees, showing the parties' final offers in relation to each head of loss together with any comments they made about each head of loss at Stage 2. Part B is a single page document which is provided to the court, in a process reminiscent of a TV game show, in a sealed envelope which is opened after the judge has made their decision. This contains each party's final offer, which can be different from the totals of each head of loss, which are treated as a form of Part 36 offer with specified consequences if beaten.

Time of payment – adults

Within 10 days of the Claimant sending a Stage 2 settlement pack the Defendant must pay the Stage 1 costs as specified at CPR r45.18 [RTA 6.18 and EL/PL 616]. The costs are set out further on in this chapter. If the Defendant fails to pay, the Claimant has 10 days to remove the claim from the Portal, after which they lose that right.

Where settlement is reached at the end of Stage 2, the Defendant must pay the costs within 10 days of the settlement [RTA 7.47 and 7.62, EL/PL 7.44]. Where settlement is not reached, the Stage 2 costs must be paid within 15 days of the receiving the Court Proceedings Pack Part A & B [RTA 7.72, EL/PL 7.55] unless the Defendant requires a new certificate of recoverable benefits, in which case they must notify the Claimant they have applied for a fresh certificate and must pay within 30 days of receiving the Court Proceedings Pack A & B [RTA

7.74, EL/PL 7.57]. The costs payable at this stage are any unpaid Stage 1 costs, Stage 2 costs, agreed disbursements. Where the amount of a disbursement is not agreed, the amount the Defendant considers reasonable must be paid [RTA 7.70 – 7.71, EL/PL 7.53 – 7.54].

Time of payment – children

The provisions of the Protocol outlined in the above section provide that where the Claimant is a child, the rules for timing of payment do not apply. For children cases, at the settlement hearing the Defendant will be ordered to pay costs pursuant to CPR r45.21 if settlement is reached at Stage 2 and if settlement is reached at Stage 3 pursuant to CPR r45.22. If no settlement is reached, then the court will order payment at the Stage 3 hearing pursuant to CPR r45.20(b)(iii).

Amounts of payment: RTA Portal

There is one dividing line when it comes to the level of Portal costs, whether the claim is over £10,000 or not. If below £10,000 the payments are as follows, set out at CPR 45.18 Table 6:

Stage 1 – £200

Stage 2 – £300

Stage 3 – Type A – £250

- Type B – £25

- Type C – £150

If above £10,000, Stage 1 & 3 costs are the same but Stage 2 costs are as follows:

Stage 2 – £600

CPR r45.18(6) confirms that VAT is recoverable in addition to the above sums, where appropriate. The main time this is likely to be of relevance is where advocates are not VAT registered.

Where the Claimant lives or works in the following areas and instructs a representative who practices in those areas, an additional 12.5% of Stage 1, 2 and 3 Type A costs are recoverable: CPR 45.18(5). The areas may change from time to time and are specified in Practice Direction 45, but at the time of writing are as follows:

> *"the area served by the County Court hearing centres at Barnet, Brentford, Central London, Clerkenwell and Shoreditch, Edmonton, Ilford, Mayors and City of London, Romford, Wandsworth and Willesden and (outside London) the County Court hearing centres at Bromley, Croydon, Dartford, Gravesend and Uxbridge."* PD 45 para 2.6.

<u>Amounts of payment: EL/PL Portal</u>

The same dividing line of £10,000 applies to the EL/PL Portal. The costs are, however, higher than the RTA Portal.

If below £10,000 the payments are as follows, set out at CPR 45.18 Table 6A:

Stage 1 – £300

Stage 2 – £600

Stage 3 – Type A – £250

- Type B – £25

- Type C – £150

If above £10,000, Stage 1 & 3 costs are the same, but Stage 2 costs are as follows:

Stage 2 – £1,300.

The same provisions as to recoverability of VAT where appropriate and 12.5% uplift for claimants and representatives in the London areas also apply.

Disbursements

Disbursements are only recoverable if specified in CPR 45.19. This rule provides:

> *(1) Subject to paragraphs (2A) to (2E), the court –*
>
> *(a) may allow a claim for a disbursement of a type mentioned in paragraphs (2) or (3); but*
>
> *(b) will not allow a claim for any other type of disbursement.*
>
> *(2) In a claim to which either the RTA Protocol or EL/PL Protocol applies, the disbursements referred to in paragraph (1) are –*
>
> *(a) the cost of obtaining –*
>
> *(i) medical records;*
>
> *(ii) a medical report or reports or non-medical expert reports as provided for in the relevant Protocol;*
>
> *(b) court fees as a result of Part 21 being applicable;*

(c) court fees payable where proceedings are started as a result of a limitation period that is about to expire;

(d) court fees in respect of the Stage 3 Procedure; and

(e) any other disbursement that has arisen due to a particular feature of the dispute.

(2A) In a soft tissue injury claim, or a claim which consists of, or includes, a claim for a whiplash injury, to which the RTA Protocol applies, the only sums (exclusive of VAT) that are recoverable in respect of the cost of obtaining a fixed cost medical report or medical records are as follows—

(a) obtaining the first report from an accredited medical expert selected via the MedCo Portal: £180;

(b) obtaining a further report where justified from an expert from one of the following disciplines—

(i) Consultant Orthopaedic Surgeon (inclusive of a review of medical records where applicable): £420;

(ii) Consultant in Accident and Emergency Medicine: £360;

(iii) General Practitioner registered with the General Medical Council: £180; or

(iv) Physiotherapist registered with the Health and Care Professions Council: £180;

(c) obtaining medical records: no more than £30 plus the direct cost from the holder of the records, and limited to £80 in total for each set of records required. Where relevant records are

required from more than one holder of records, the fixed fee applies to each set of records required;

(d) addendum report on medical records (except by Consultant Orthopaedic Surgeon): £50; and

(e) answer to questions under Part 35: £80.

(2B) Save in exceptional circumstances, no fee may be allowed for the cost of obtaining a report to which paragraph (2A) applies where the medical expert—

(a) has provided treatment to the claimant;

(b) is associated with any person who has provided treatment; or

(c) proposes or recommends treatment that they or an associate then provide.

(2C) The cost of obtaining a further report from an expert not listed in paragraph (2A)(b) is not fixed, but the use of that expert and the cost must be justified.

(2D) Where appropriate, VAT may be recovered in addition to the cost of obtaining a fixed cost medical report or medical records.

(2E) In this rule, 'accredited medical expert', 'associate', 'associated with', 'fixed cost medical report' 'MedCo', soft tissue injury claim' and 'whiplash injury' have the same meaning as in paragraph 1.1(A1), (1A), (10A), (12A), and (16A) and (20A), respectively, of the RTA Protocol.

(3) In a claim to which the RTA Protocol applies, the disbursements referred to in paragraph (1) are also the cost of—

(a) an engineer's report; and

(b) a search of the records of the—

(i) Driver Vehicle Licensing Authority; and

(ii) Motor Insurance Database.

It largely mirrors r45.29I and so the guidance in relation to that rule earlier in this book will be of assistance.

The main changes are that there is a reference to the court fees arising from Part 21 being applicable, i.e. where the claim is issued for approval of a child's claim and where limitation is about to expire. This latter element arises from paragraphs 5.7 – 5.8 of both the RTA Protocol and EL/PL Protocol, together with Practice Direction 8B paragraph 16, which allows a claimant to issue and seek a stay if limitation will expire prior to settlement at Stage 2 or the start of Stage 3.

Additional advice

It is possible to recover from the defendant the costs of an additional advice reasonably required to value the claim. That is provided for by r45.23B. It only applies to claims where the value is more than £10,000. The sum is fixed at £150, being the Stage 3 Type C cost.

Cases including children

These cases come with their own specific rules, largely directed at the need for any settlement to be approved by the court under CPR Pt 21.

CPR r45.21 applies where a child's claim is settled at Stage 2. It must then be issued for an approval. The claimant is entitled at the approval hearing to the full Stage 1-3 costs including Types A, B and C, together with any disbursements under r45.19.

If the settlement is not approved, then the court will order the payment of Stage 1 and Stage 2 costs, per r45.21(3).

If the settlement is approved at a second settlement hearing then subparagraph (5) provides that the claimant is entitled to Stage 3 Type A, B and C costs plus disbursements. The court also has the power under subparagraph (6) to order at its discretion that either the defendant or the claimant pay an additional amount of Stage 3 Type A and/or Type B costs.

The situation where a child's case settles for an amount more than the defendant's offer but after proceedings are started under Stage 3 is covered by r45.22. This largely mirrors r45.21 save that a subparagraph 7 provides that *"Where the settlement is not approved at the Stage 3 hearing the court will order the defendant to pay the Stage 3 Type A fixed costs."*

PD8B paragraphs 3.3 and 3.4 provides definitions for 'settlement hearing' and 'Stage 3 hearing'. It is difficult to envisage exactly what this element is aimed at, because a 'Stage 3 hearing' is defined as *"a final hearing to determine the amount of damages that remain in dispute between the parties."* Presumably it means where *some* items have been settled but not all of them, such that the approval is needed for those items not in dispute but is not provided by the court.

Not continuing under Stage 3

For children, under r45.23, if the court determines that the Stage 3 process is not appropriate for the settlement or contested damages determination the court will order the defendant to pay Stage 1-3 including Types A – C costs.

In adult cases, PD8B paragraph 7.3 provides that the court will not allow Stage 3 costs.

Settlement after Stage 2 – adult

This is covered, at least in part, by r45.23A. That rule applies where a settlement is agreed at more than the defendant's protocol offer, after the Court Proceedings Pack has been sent but before the claim is issued. In that scenario the claimant is also entitled to Stage 3 Type A costs.

Where the claim is settled after issue of the claim then r45.25 applies. Subparagraph (1) states that the rule is said to apply where an application is made to determine the costs under r45.29. That cannot be right insofar as it appears to limit the application, because r45.29(3) itself states that the court will apply r45.25 (or r45.22 for children) where such a costs application is made. It would otherwise mean that a claimant (or defendant) would be obliged to issue a costs only to unlock the costs under r45.25, requiring more use of court time and resources.

That potential, albeit hopefully unnecessary, controversy aside, r45.25 provides that where the settlement is more than the defendant's protocol offer the claimant is entitled to Stage 1, Stage 2 and Stage 3 Type A costs and disbursements under r45.19. Where the settlement is less than or equal to the defendant's protocol offer then the court will order the payment of Stage 1 and Stage 2 costs plus disbursements allowed under r45.19.

The court may also order either party to pay the costs of the application, although no amount appears fixed.

<u>Protocol offers</u>

A protocol offer is defined by CPR r36.25 as the total final amount of the offers from both parties as recorded in the Court Proceedings Pack Part B. It must be the final offer made at Stage 2 [RTA 7.64(2)(b) and EL/PL 7.48(b)].

The offer is deemed to be made on the first business day after the Court Proceedings Pack is sent to the defendant, per r.36.26.

Where the claimant fails to beat the defendant's protocol offer then r36.29(2) provides the claimant must pay the costs set out in r45.26, namely Stage 3 Type A costs if determined on the papers and Type A and B costs if determined at a hearing. The claimant must also pay interest on those fixed costs from the date of the offer. The rate of interest is not actually specified by the rule, but the courts apply by analogy the "*a rate not exceeding 10% above base rate*" that is provided for when a claimant beats their offer. The defendant is also entitled to any disbursements under r45.19.

Where the claimant beats the defendant's protocol offer then the claimant is simply entitled to the Stage 1-3 costs and disbursements as set out already.

Where the claimant beats its own protocol offer, then r36.29(4) provides that the claimant gets the Stage 1- 3 costs and disbursements as set out above and interest on those costs for all or some of the period from the date of the protocol offer. The claimant also gets interest on damages and an uplift of 10% on the damages.

Adjournment

If a settlement hearing or Stage 3 hearing is adjourned, r45.27 provides that the court has a discretion to order either party to pay an amount of Stage 3 Type B costs and any court fee for that adjournment. The Type B costs are of course £250.

Interim hearings

The rules do not provide for interim hearing fees in portal cases. They do, however, arise. It is the practice of most courts to allow the same £250 interim hearing costs. This is arguably contrary to r45.17 which provides that the *only costs* allowed are those provided for within the rules. No such provision does appear.

Costs disputes

If a costs dispute arises then if the claim is issued r45.29 applies. If the claim is not issued then, at least in relation to disbursements, in RTA cases the protocol states that a party can use r45.29 [RTA 7.45]. By contrast, in EL/PL cases it is said that r46.14 is applicable [EL/PL 46.14]. The reason for this distinction is not clear.

MORE BOOKS BY LAW BRIEF PUBLISHING

'Covid-19, Homeworking and the Law – The Essential Guide to Employment and GDPR Issues' by Forbes Solicitors
'Covid-19, Force Majeure and Frustration of Contracts – The Essential Guide' by Keith Markham
'Covid-19 and Criminal Law – The Essential Guide' by Ramya Nagesh
'Covid-19 and Family Law in England and Wales – The Essential Guide' by Safda Mahmood
'A Practical Guide to the Law of Unlawful Eviction and Harassment – 2nd Edition' by Stephanie Lovegrove
'Covid-19, Residential Property, Equity Release and Enfranchisement – The Essential Guide' by Paul Sams and Louise Uphill
'Covid-19, Brexit and the Law of Commercial Leases – The Essential Guide' by Mark Shelton
'A Practical Guide to Costs in Personal Injury Claims – 2nd Edition' by Matthew Hoe
'A Practical Guide to the General Data Protection Regulation (GDPR) – 2nd Edition' by Keith Markham
'Ellis on Credit Hire – Sixth Edition' by Aidan Ellis & Tim Kevan
'A Practical Guide to Working with Litigants in Person and McKenzie Friends in Family Cases' by Stuart Barlow
'Protecting Unregistered Brands: A Practical Guide to the Law of Passing Off' by Lorna Brazell
'A Practical Guide to Secondary Liability and Joint Enterprise Post-Jogee' by Joanne Cecil & James Mehigan
'A Practical Guide to the Pre-Action RTA Claims Protocol for Personal Injury Lawyers' by Antonia Ford
'A Practical Guide to Neighbour Disputes and the Law' by Alexander Walsh
'A Practical Guide to Forfeiture of Leases' by Mark Shelton
'A Practical Guide to Coercive Control for Legal Practitioners and Victims' by Rachel Horman

'A Practical Guide to Rights Over Airspace and Subsoil' by Daniel Gatty
'Tackling Disclosure in the Criminal Courts – A Practitioner's Guide' by Narita Bahra QC & Don Ramble
'A Practical Guide to the Law of Driverless Cars – Second Edition' by Alex Glassbrook, Emma Northey & Scarlett Milligan
'A Practical Guide to TOLATA Claims' by Greg Williams
'Artificial Intelligence – The Practical Legal Issues' by John Buyers
'A Practical Guide to the Law of Prescription in Scotland' by Andrew Foyle
'A Practical Guide to the Construction and Rectification of Wills and Trust Instruments' by Edward Hewitt
'A Practical Guide to the Law of Bullying and Harassment in the Workplace' by Philip Hyland
'How to Be a Freelance Solicitor: A Practical Guide to the SRA-Regulated Freelance Solicitor Model' by Paul Bennett
'A Practical Guide to Prison Injury Claims' by Malcolm Johnson
'A Practical Guide to the Small Claims Track' by Dominic Bright
'A Practical Guide to Advising Clients at the Police Station' by Colin Stephen McKeown-Beaumont
'A Practical Guide to Antisocial Behaviour Injunctions' by Iain Wightwick
'Practical Mediation: A Guide for Mediators, Advocates, Advisers, Lawyers, and Students in Civil, Commercial, Business, Property, Workplace, and Employment Cases' by Jonathan Dingle with John Sephton
'The Mini-Pupillage Workbook' by David Boyle
'A Practical Guide to Crofting Law' by Brian Inkster
'A Practical Guide to Spousal Maintenance' by Liz Cowell
'A Practical Guide to the Law of Domain Names and Cybersquatting' by Andrew Clemson
'A Practical Guide to the Law of Gender Pay Gap Reporting' by Harini Iyengar

'A Practical Guide to the Rights of Grandparents in Children Proceedings' by Stuart Barlow
'NHS Whistleblowing and the Law' by Joseph England
'Employment Law and the Gig Economy' by Nigel Mackay & Annie Powell
'A Practical Guide to Noise Induced Hearing Loss (NIHL) Claims' by Andrew Mckie, Ian Skeate, Gareth McAloon
'An Introduction to Beauty Negligence Claims – A Practical Guide for the Personal Injury Practitioner' by Greg Almond
'Intercompany Agreements for Transfer Pricing Compliance' by Paul Sutton
'Zen and the Art of Mediation' by Martin Plowman
'A Practical Guide to the SRA Principles, Individual and Law Firm Codes of Conduct 2019 – What Every Law Firm Needs to Know' by Paul Bennett
'A Practical Guide to Adoption for Family Lawyers' by Graham Pegg
'A Practical Guide to Industrial Disease Claims' by Andrew Mckie & Ian Skeate
'A Practical Guide to Redundancy' by Philip Hyland
'A Practical Guide to Vicarious Liability' by Mariel Irvine
'A Practical Guide to Applications for Landlord's Consent and Variation of Leases' by Mark Shelton
'A Practical Guide to Relief from Sanctions Post-Mitchell and Denton' by Peter Causton
'A Practical Guide to Equity Release for Advisors' by Paul Sams
'A Practical Guide to the Law Relating to Food' by Ian Thomas
'A Practical Guide to Financial Services Claims' by Chris Hegarty
'The Law of Houses in Multiple Occupation: A Practical Guide to HMO Proceedings' by Julian Hunt
'A Practical Guide to Unlawful Eviction and Harassment' by Stephanie Lovegrove
'Occupiers, Highways and Defective Premises Claims: A Practical Guide Post-Jackson – 2nd Edition' by Andrew Mckie

www.ingramcontent.com/pod-product-compliance
Lightning Source LLC
LaVergne TN
LVHW022305200926
848481LV00004B/1223